Original title:
Winter's Whisper

Author: Liisi Lendorav
ISBN HARDBACK: 978-9916-79-786-0
ISBN PAPERBACK: 978-9916-79-787-7
ISBN EBOOK: 978-9916-79-788-4

Secrets in the Silence

In the hush of night, whispers dwell,
Hidden tales that silence can tell.
Stars above, they softly gleam,
Carrying shadows of a dream.

Through the echoes, heartbeats sway,
Lingering thoughts in disarray.
Words unspoken, lost in air,
Secrets linger, laid bare.

Life's soft murmur, a fleeting song,
In stillness, where we all belong.
Quiet moments, hearts align,
Finding truths in space divine.

The world outside may rush and race,
But in the calm, we find our place.
A gentle breeze, sweetened sigh,
Whispers of love that never die.

Beneath the surface, deep and wide,
Where mystery and magic reside.
In the silence, fears dissolve,
A sacred space where souls evolve.

Choreography of Frost

In the quiet morn, light unfolds,
Frost on branches, a tale retold.
Delicate crystals, dance in grace,
Nature's ballet, a frozen embrace.

Each step whispers, secrets held tight,
A tranquil world, bathed in white.
The air sparkles, bright with cheer,
As winter's canvas, draws us near.

Footprints trace, a path anew,
In a realm where wishes come true.
With every breath, see the magic glow,
In this choreography, we let go.

Calm amidst the Cold

Silent moments, the world at rest,
Wrapped in layers, we feel blessed.
Snowflakes whisper, softly they fall,
Creating peace, a soothing call.

A distant hearth, with flames aglow,
Warmth within, while cold winds blow.
Blankets of white, drape the earth,
A gentle hug, in winter's birth.

Here in stillness, hearts unite,
Finding solace, through the night.
With every breath, we share our dreams,
In this calm, life brightly beams.

Vows in the Snow

Under the boughs, where shadows play,
Promises linger, come what may.
Snowflakes witness the vows we make,
In the chill, our hearts awake.

With laughter ringing, joy resounds,
In the silence, love abounds.
Together we carve, our names in time,
In purest white, a love sublime.

Around us swirls, the winter breath,
But in our hearts, there's no such depth.
We stand entwined, in soft moonlight,
Our vows aglow, in the coming night.

Murmurs of the North Wind

Whispers of frost, in twilight's glow,
The north wind carries tales of snow.
With every gust, a story spins,
Of ancient lands, where silence begins.

Between the pines, secrets weave,
In the chill, we learn to believe.
Echoes of laughter, carried afar,
Guiding us home, like a northern star.

Beneath the sky, where true hearts soar,
The murmurs of winter, call us for more.
In their embrace, we find our way,
With the north wind’s song, we gently sway.

Midnight Chill

The moon hangs low, a silver glow,
Whispers of night in shadows flow.
Stars blink above, so far, so near,
Quiet moments hold us here.

A breath of wind, a soft embrace,
Coolness wraps around this place.
Footsteps fade on icy ground,
Midnight whispers all around.

Darkness deepens, time stands still,
Hearts awake to winter's thrill.
The air carries a timeless song,
In this stillness, we belong.

Frosted branches, trees so bare,
Wonders hidden everywhere.
Nature sleeps in crystal light,
Wrapped in dreams of silent night.

Moments linger, shadows play,
Night shall gently fade away.
But till dawn, we breathe it in,
This midnight chill beneath our skin.

Frosted Sighs

A breath escapes in frosty air,
Capturing moments, fragile care.
Each sigh a whisper, soft and clear,
Echoes of winter drawing near.

The world adorned in shimmering white,
Frosted landscapes under moonlight.
Trees stand tall in silent grace,
Nature's canvas, a serene space.

Footprints traced on icy ground,
In every corner, magic found.
Softly spoken, the night replies,
With gentle warmth, these frosted sighs.

Stars twinkle like diamonds above,
Wrapped in the stillness of love.
A moment paused, a heart set free,
In winter's breath, just you and me.

As dawn approaches, colors blend,
The frost may fade, but hearts won't end.
In every sigh, a story lies,
Held close within these frosted skies.

The Stillness Between Storms

Calm prevails, the sky so gray,
Hushed are the winds that sway.
Clouds gather low, a heavy veil,
In this stillness, we set sail.

Birds find rest on branches bare,
Nature breathes with gentle care.
Moments linger, shadows creep,
In between, our promises keep.

The world prepares for thunder's call,
Yet in this pause, we feel it all.
Whispers ride on muted air,
Love is found, and hearts laid bare.

Lightning flickers in the deep,
An electric charge where memories sleep.
Yet for now, we dance with time,
In this stillness, everything's fine.

Embrace the calm, let worries part,
For storms may pass, but love's an art.
Between each tempest, find your way,
In stillness, let your spirit stay.

Hoarfrost Murmurs

Morning breaks with frosted lace,
Nature whispers of her grace.
Each branch kissed in icy glow,
Hoarfrost murmurs soft and low.

The ground is still, a silent quilt,
Each crystal formed, as if by guilt.
Murmurs echo in the chill,
Winter’s heart beats strong and still.

Sunrise paints the world anew,
Glistening diamonds in every view.
A serenade to the waking light,
Leaving shadows of the night.

In every nook, a story gleams,
Hoarfrost whispers of hidden dreams.
We walk through magic, hand in hand,
A world transformed by winter’s strand.

So let the cold embrace our souls,
In hoarfrost murmurs, time unfolds.
With winter’s breath, our hearts align,
In nature’s dance, our spirits shine.

The Grasp of Gray

Whispers of fog in the dawn's light,
Shadows stretch long, fading from sight.
Each breath a chill, rising and slow,
Lost in the grasp of the ashen glow.

Trees stand silent, their branches bare,
A world cloaked in somber despair.
Ghosts of the past softly weave,
In the heart of gray, I grieve.

Time dances soft where the shadows play,
Colors dim with a hint of decay.
I wander through dreams of the light,
In the grasp of gray, surrendering to night.

Shards of Ice and Solitude

Crystals fall like broken glass,
Each shard a moment that will not pass.
In the stillness, echoes ring clear,
Silhouettes whisper, yet no one is near.

Frost-laden branches that tremble and shake,
Carry the weight of the choices we make.
Cold breaths linger, heavy with doubt,
In solitude's grasp, we drift about.

Mirrored reflections in a frozen stream,
Capture the fragments of dreams once gleam.
In the distance, a lone bird calls,
Amidst shards of ice, its weary heart stalls.

Northern Mists

Veils of mist cling to the trees,
A haunting beauty, a ghostly freeze.
Shadows dance under silver clouds,
Wraps the world in silence, shrouds.

Footsteps muffled on the damp ground,
In the northern mists, peace is found.
Whispers of nature weave through the air,
A promise of magic, a moment rare.

The horizon blurs where the sky meets land,
Lost in the softness, I make my stand.
In the embrace of the cool, gentle mist,
My heart finds solace, a quiet tryst.

Beneath a Blanket of Snow

Softly it falls, the world turns white,
A blanket of snow that hushes the night.
Every sound muffled, every edge blurred,
Under the dome, peace is stirred.

Footprints emerge on the pristine ground,
Each step a story, quiet, profound.
A canvas of dreams in winter's embrace,
Beneath the snow, time finds its pace.

The stars peek through, twinkling and bright,
In the stillness, they kindle the night.
Wrapped in the warmth of the stars above,
Beneath a blanket, I feel your love.

Serene Snowscapes

In the hush of gentle night,
Snowflakes dance in silver light.
Blanket soft, the world transformed,
Nature's peace, a heart warmed.

Whispers float on frosty air,
Trees adorned, a beauty rare.
Footprints tread on purest white,
Serenading winter's quiet plight.

Moonbeams cast a tranquil glow,
Reflecting all the dreams below.
Somewhere deep, a stillness hums,
In snowscapes where the silence comes.

Icicles cling like crystal tears,
Holding close the fleeting years.
Time moves slow in this embrace,
Forever caught in winter's grace.

Each breath released, a fleeting mist,
In the chill, there’s warmth persist.
Snowflakes fall, a soft ballet,
Serene snowscapes hold their sway.

Frost Bloom

Morning breaks in frosted hues,
Nature wakes with gentle views.
Petals wrapped in icy lace,
Frost blooms in a wintry space.

Sunlight glimmers on the ground,
In this magic, joy is found.
Each blade shimmers, whispering light,
A crystalline, enchanting sight.

Birdsongs float through silver skies,
As winter's heart gently sighs.
Life holds on in secret ways,
In frost bloom's soft, tender gaze.

Frozen wonders grace the trees,
Kissing air with soothing breeze.
Branches wear their diamond crowns,
In beauty, winter gently drowns.

Hope awakens with the dawn,
In every frost, a promise drawn.
Nature's artistry unfolds,
In winter’s grip, a warmth enfolds.

Silent Frost

Silent frost, a veiled embrace,
Touching all with gentle grace.
Nature pauses, breath held tight,
In the stillness of the night.

Whispers linger in the air,
Silent moments, pure and rare.
Where shadows play on snowy ground,
In silence, magic shall be found.

Stars above in twilight glow,
Casting light on all below.
Frosted whispers, secrets kept,
In winter's arms, the world has slept.

Beneath the chill, life lies awake,
In quietude, the heart won't break.
Hope endures in frosted dreams,
Where silence flows like silver streams.

Every flake a story told,
Silent frost, a beauty bold.
In frozen realms, a peace prevails,
Where winter's breath softly exhales.

A Breath of Ice

A breath of ice, a whispered sigh,
Frosty air where stillness lies.
Nature wrapped in purest white,
A canvas smooth, a tranquil sight.

Snowflakes waltz on zephyr's breeze,
Painting dreams on barren trees.
Every flake a tale to weave,
In the hush, we dare believe.

Crystal shards in morning light,
Sparkling gems, a heart's delight.
With every step, the world awakes,
In the chill, a soul remakes.

As shadows stretch and daylight creeps,
Winter's promise gently keeps.
A breath of ice, a calming gift,
In the cold, our spirits lift.

Together, we embrace the freeze,
In winter’s charm, we find our ease.
For every sigh that slips from lips,
A breath of ice, the heart eclipses.

Nature's Stillframe

In the woods where silence lingers,
Soft whispers dance on gentle streams.
Leaves rustle with the song of fingers,
Life unfolds in sunlit dreams.

Mountains stand like ancient towers,
Guardians of the tranquil lands.
Petals bow to fragrant flowers,
Nature’s art rests in steady hands.

Morning breaks with golden light,
Birds awaken, sweetly soar.
In this moment, pure delight,
Every sight, a love encore.

Clouds drift slow in skies so blue,
Casting shadows earthward drawn.
Hues of nature, rich and true,
Paint the canvas of the dawn.

Silent echoes fill the air,
As daylight fades and night awakes.
Stars emerge, a glimmered fair,
In stillframes, serenity makes.

The Serene Blanket

A quilt of green beneath my feet,
Soft moss cushions every step.
Whispers travel, subtle, sweet,
Nature's secret, softly kept.

The brook hums a soothing tune,
Beneath the shade of ancient trees.
Where petals fall like drops of noon,
And wanderers find gentle peace.

Sunbeams weave through branches high,
Painting shadows on the ground.
In this haven, time drifts by,
Where silence sings, no harsher sound.

A breeze stirs the fragrant air,
With hints of pine and wildflower.
Wrapped in nature’s tender care,
Each moment cherished, hour by hour.

As twilight folds the day away,
Stars ignite the velvet sky.
In the still, I long to stay,
Under nature’s watchful eye.

Crystalline Imagery

Glistening shards of morning dew,
Crystals formed where sunlight bends.
Nature's jewels, pure and true,
Each drop a story that transcends.

Frosted windows greet the dawn,
Patterns lace like whispered dreams.
Beauty found in every lawn,
Where light and shadow softly gleam.

A snowflake's dance, a fleeting breath,
Unique and transient, art divine.
In winter's chill, a life meets death,
Yet beauty thrives in perfect line.

Icicles hang like crystal swords,
Awaiting sun to bid adieu.
Nature sketches with her chords,
In every form, a world anew.

When evening falls, reflections glow,
Mirrored skies of twilight's grace.
Crystalline imagery flows,
In stillness, find a sacred space.

Icicle Dreams

Icicles dangle from the eaves,
Glistening in the winter light.
Fragile dreams that nature weaves,
Hanging crystal, pure and bright.

Each drop like a story untold,
Reflecting hopes beneath the sun.
In their beauty, hearts unfold,
A quiet chorus, softly sung.

Beneath the weight of winter's chill,
The world wears a shimmery gown.
In this freeze, a moment still,
Time holds fast, no need to frown.

Stars above in frosty skies,
Mirror the beauty down below.
In this scene where silence lies,
Icicle dreams in soft, white glow.

As the seasons start to change,
Gentle thaw will come to greet.
Yet in this icy, sweet exchange,
Memories of winter, bittersweet.

Fragments of a Frostbitten Night

Whispers of the cold wind call,
Stars glimmer, tiny and small.
Moonlight dances on icy streams,
Shattering the night's dark dreams.

Footprints linger in the snow,
Silent tales of those who go.
Each breath a fleeting, chilling mist,
In this frost, moments persist.

Branches creak, the forest sighs,
Wrapped in winter's soft disguise.
Nature's breath, a frosty kiss,
In the stillness, there's a bliss.

Glances to a distant past,
Memories in twilight cast.
Frosted echoes, shadows play,
In the night, they drift away.

A shiver runs through timeless trees,
As cold as ancient, whispered pleas.
Fragments of a silent night,
Frostbitten dreams take flight.

The Calm of Snowfall

Softly dances, flakes descend,
Nature's blanket, white, extends.
Silence wraps the world in peace,
Winter's charm, a sweet release.

Each flake tells a story new,
Cradled gently, kissed by dew.
Moments woven, pure, and bright,
In the calm of winter's night.

Hushed are voices, still the air,
As beauty lingers everywhere.
Footsteps muffled in this dream,
Life, it seems, is but a gleam.

Time slows down, the world awaits,
While snow decorates the gates.
Branches bow with heavy grace,
In this tranquil, snowy space.

Not a sound, just pure delight,
In the calm, the stars ignite.
Everything feels so serene,
Wrapped in winter's loving sheen.

Thawing Shadows

Winter wanes, the sun creeps near,
Life returns, dispelling fear.
Icicles drip, a gentle sigh,
Shadows stretch beneath the sky.

Colors melt from gray to gold,
Stories of the earth unfold.
In the glow of warming rays,
Nature wakes from cold's deep haze.

Streams begin to hum and flow,
Chasing off the winter's glow.
Animals emerge to play,
Chasing shadows of the day.

Buds burst forth with vibrant cheer,
Whispers of the coming year.
Dancing light, a joyful sound,
In the thaw, new life is found.

As the icy grip releases,
Springtime's promise never ceases.
Shadows soft in golden light,
Thawing whispers, warm and bright.

The Silent Grove

Deep within the forest green,
Lies a place where few have been.
Trees stand tall, a stoic line,
Guardians of secrets divine.

In the stillness, whispers hum,
Nature's pulse, a steady drum.
Leaves like velvet, soft and light,
In the grove, the world feels right.

Sunlight dapples through the boughs,
In quiet grace, the forest bows.
Meet the silence, let it grow,
In the heart of the grove's glow.

Mossy carpets hug the ground,
Life in shadows, peace is found.
Stories told in rustling leaves,
In the grove where nature weaves.

Time stands still in this embrace,
Wildflower dances, soft and grace.
In the silent grove we see,
Endless wonder, wild and free.

Frosty Gazes

In the morning light, so bright,
Frost sparkles on leaves, a sight.
Eyes wide with wonder and glee,
Nature whispers a soft decree.

Breeses carry secrets untold,
In the silence, the world feels bold.
Every breath, a clouded sigh,
Making magic in the sky.

Children laugh, they dance and play,
In the frost, they find their way.
Snowflakes falling, a gentle kiss,
Moments wrapped in winter's bliss.

Creatures scurry, seeking warmth,
Nature's chill, a soft alarm.
With frosty gazes, we stand still,
Capturing dreams in the winter chill.

As twilight falls, the stars appear,
Softly glowing, they draw near.
In the night's embrace, we wander,
Through frosty gazes, we ponder.

The Slumbering Landscape

Snow blankets the fields, serene,
A quiet hush, a gentle sheen.
Trees stand tall, draped in white,
Guardians of the peaceful night.

Hills roll softly, curves in sleep,
A world wrapped in dreams so deep.
Moonlight dances on frozen streams,
Chasing shadows of whispered dreams.

Animal tracks lead the way,
Stories told of their play.
In the stillness, life unfolds,
Nature's secrets, softly told.

Each breath, a mist, a fleeting trace,
In this slumbering, tranquil space.
Time slows down, as we explore,
The beauty of winter, we adore.

With hearts aglow and spirits light,
We wander through the velvet night.
In the landscape, a gentle sigh,
Embraced beneath a starlit sky.

Chill in the Air

A chill in the air, crisp and clear,
Whispers of winter drawing near.
Breath turns to steam, a fleeting cloud,
Nature wraps us in her shroud.

Scattered leaves dance in the breeze,
With every gust, they clamber with ease.
Branches creak, secrets resonate,
In the chill, we contemplate.

Fires crackle, warmth draws us close,
In this season, we cherish most.
Cocoa steaming in our hands,
Shared laughter, as warmth expands.

Frosted windows, a canvas bright,
Dancing shadows in the night.
With every moment, we embrace,
The chill in the air, a sweet grace.

As daylight fades, the stars awake,
In the chill, our hearts do take.
Moments linger, a special kind,
In the chill, true joy we find.

Pastel Skies

The horizon blushes with morning light,
Pastel hues inviting flight.
Peach and lavender blend and swirl,
In the sky, a gentle unfurl.

Clouds drift softly, painted dreams,
In twilight's glow, the beauty beams.
A canvas vast, where whispers arise,
In the embrace of pastel skies.

Birds take wing, a graceful dance,
Soaring high, they find their chance.
Winds carry songs, sweet and soft,
In the warmth, our spirits lift off.

As sunlight fades to deep indigo,
The stars awaken, a radiant glow.
In these moments, love takes flight,
Beneath the pastel cloak of night.

With every dawn, a fresh surprise,
Endless beauty in pastel skies.
We find our dreams and let them soar,
In nature's art, forevermore.

The Quietude of Frost

In the stillness of the night,
a blanket white unfurls,
trees stand wrapped in soft embrace,
time in quiet whirls.

Moonlight dances on the ground,
shimmers glow like dreams,
breathing in the frozen air,
everything is as it seems.

Footsteps crunch on powdered paths,
gentle whispers call,
every flake a story told,
in nature's silent thrall.

Wonders hide in frost-kissed leaves,
a symphony of peace,
where winter weaves its tapestry,
and all the chaos cease.

Embrace the quietude around,
let serenity unfold,
for in the frosty morning light,
new tales begin, retold.

Numbed Dreams

In the depths of winter's grasp,
where warmth is a distant dream,
a fragile heart beats slowly,
adrift in a hallowed gleam.

Veils of white conceal the past,
dreams buried in the snow,
like whispers lost to cold embrace,
awaiting spring’s warm glow.

Stars above, they shimmer faint,
like visions in the night,
every hope a distant flame,
surrounded, yet out of sight.

Frosty breath hangs in the air,
thoughts linger, softly spun,
a tapestry of numbed desires,
beneath the winter sun.

Yet in the stillness, sparks ignite,
between the silent sighs,
a promise of the thawing warmth,
as seasons rise and fly.

A Veil of Stillness

A curtain drawn in silver light,
a blanket soft and pale,
the world beneath a gentle sheet,
a whisper on the gale.

Each flake that falls, a quiet thought,
that dances with the breeze,
a moment frozen in your hand,
where worries come to cease.

Branches glisten, bending low,
as if to touch the ground,
while shadows stretch in silent grace,
where tranquil dreams are found.

The air is thick with fragrant calm,
a stillness, deep and clear,
every heartbeat echoes soft,
each breath a reminder here.

Within this veil of pristine white,
let burdens fade away,
for in this tranquil, fleeting space,
we find our souls at play.

Frosty Echoes

Echoes dance in frosty air,
a symphony so bright,
each note a shiver on the skin,
a wonder wrapped in night.

The ground beneath a crystal quilt,
in patterns soft and deep,
the chill that lingers in the breeze,
wakes memories from sleep.

Voices carried on the wind,
soft murmurs, faintly heard,
a dialogue of winter's heart,
where every sound's a word.

In gardens dressed in icy hues,
a tapestry of light,
frosty echoes sing their songs,
in velvet cloaks of white.

So step into this frozen realm,
let magic intertwine,
for in the chill, the heart finds warmth,
in every frosty line.

Whispers of the Frost

In the quiet of the night,
Frost whispers soft and low,
A chill wraps around,
Like dreams that gently flow.

Moonlight casts a silver hue,
Kissing the frozen ground,
Each crystal sparkles bright,
In silence, beauty found.

Trees wear coats of icy lace,
Branches heavy with the weight,
Nature's art, so pure, so still,
A moment to celebrate.

Breath hangs like mist in air,
In the cold, we find our place,
Frosty whispers linger long,
In winter's soft embrace.

As dawn breaks with a blush,
Chill retreats, but memories stay,
Whispers of the frost remain,
In hearts, they softly play.

Glittering Drift

Snowflakes dance upon the breeze,
Twinkling in the morning light,
A glittering drift unfolds,
A wondrous, sparkling sight.

Children laugh, their spirits soar,
As they tread on soft, white bliss,
Building castles in the snow,
Sealing winter with a kiss.

Trees adorned, a frosty crown,
Nature's jewelry shines bright,
Underneath a quilt of white,
In the calm of winter's night.

Footprints mark the path we take,
Each step a story, freshly told,
In the drift, we find our joy,
In the chill, our hearts feel bold.

As the sunset paints the sky,
Golden hues on silver ground,
The world transformed, enchanted dreams,
In this glittering drift, we're bound.

The Lounge of Snow

Softly falls the snow tonight,
Cocooning all in white,
In the lounge of winter's breath,
We find our sweet delight.

Fires crackle, warmth does flow,
Outside, a world so still,
Inside, laughter, stories shared,
With hearts that winter fill.

Candles flicker, shadows dance,
In this cozy, glowing space,
Snowflakes waltz upon the ledge,
Adorning each window place.

Mugs of cocoa, marshmallows melt,
As dreams unfold and play,
In the lounge of snow and warmth,
We'll linger there and stay.

Morning light will soon appear,
But for now, let's cherish slow,
Together here, in winter's hug,
In the lounge, with love, we glow.

A Glacial Embrace

A touch of frost upon the earth,
A glacial embrace unfolds,
Nature's breath, so crisp and fresh,
As winter's tale is told.

Mountains draped in icy white,
Majestic, standing tall,
Whispers of the ancient past,
In frozen silence call.

Rivers wrapped in crystal sheets,
Flowing like dreams afar,
In the stillness, beauty reigns,
Beneath the evening star.

Time slows down in winter's grasp,
As we wander through the cold,
Every corner filled with light,
And stories to unfold.

As daylight fades and shadows shift,
In the chill, we find our grace,
Held within a loving hush,
In nature’s glacial embrace.

Solitary Solstices

In twilight hours, shadows blend,
Lonely whispers, the night will send.
A quiet glow from stars above,
Silent echoes of forgotten love.

The moon it glows, a silver round,
In stillness here, no other sound.
Each heartbeat feels like time stands still,
In solitude, I seek my will.

A breath of frost upon my skin,
The dance of silence, I begin.
With every moment, shadows play,
A fleeting thought, then slips away.

The seasons change, yet I remain,
In quiet paths, I know my pain.
With winter’s touch, a chill runs deep,
In solitude, these thoughts I keep.

Yet in this hush, a spark ignites,
Through solitude, my spirit fights.
From depth of night, a dawn will rise,
To warm the heart and clear the skies.

Muffled Trails of the Cold

Footsteps crunch on frosty ground,
Silence wraps the world around.
The air is sharp, the sky is gray,
In winter's grip, the trees sway.

Muffled sounds in twilight's breath,
Whispers dance with thoughts of death.
Each step forward, the chill clings tight,
Guiding me through the thick of night.

Underneath a blanket white,
Nature sleeps, lost to the night.
With every drift, the memories fade,
In hushed tones, my fears are laid.

Cold winds howl, a voice unseen,
Through the frozen fields of green.
In this quiet, I seek a sign,
To lead me through this space divine.

Yet beauty lurks in frosty halls,
Winter's breath in gentle calls.
With every pause, I find my grace,
In muffled trails, I find my place.

The Essence of Chill

Whispers of dusk in chilling air,
A tranquil touch that lingers there.
The essence of cold, a haunting sigh,
Where dreams take flight and shadows fly.

Frost-kissed leaves, the world in white,
Every corner holds the night.
In silence deep, reflections gleam,
In winter's grasp, we dare to dream.

The stars shimmer, a distant call,
Through frosty breath, I feel it all.
As stillness reigns, time drifts apart,
Each icy moment, a work of art.

In the heart of chill, warmth may grow,
Amidst the frost, life flows slow.
For hidden beneath the cold exterior,
Hope lingers softly, a bright carrier.

So let the chill embrace the night,
Within the darkness, find the light.
For in the essence of this freeze,
We learn to listen, find our peace.

The Softest Blanket

In the quiet night sky, soft and deep,
A blanket of stars, secrets to keep.
Whispers of warmth, in shadows they play,
Cradling the world, till the break of day.

Gentle the touch of the winter's grace,
Covering fields in a shimmering lace.
Each flake a promise, each flake a dream,
Wrapped in the stillness, in moonlight’s beam.

Beneath the soft layer, life starts to sigh,
Every breath a snowflake, drifting by.
Hidden are stories, in white they unfold,
A magic that dances, a tale retold.

As night draws near, and shadows grow long,
The blanket of peace hums a gentle song.
Hearts gather close, beneath the night’s glow,
In the softest embrace, love continues to grow.

Snowflakes' Lullaby

Listen to the whispers of the falling snow,
Each flake a melody, gentle and slow.
They twirl and they drift, a ballet of white,
Softly they blanket the world in the night.

The wind plays the tune as the stars softly shine,
A lullaby sung in the sweet, frosty pine.
With each gentle touch, the earth takes a breath,
Cradled in winter, a dance with sweet death.

While shadows grow long and the day fades away,
The snowflakes gather, at the close of the day.
Each crystal a note in the night's quiet hymn,
Playing a song where the dark skies are dim.

A symphony woven, with shimmering light,
Through the stillness, it echoes, a pure delight.
Beneath this soft blanket of silence so deep,
The world finds its rest, as it drifts into sleep.

Frigid Dreams

In the stillest moment, when breath fogs the air,
Frigid dreams wander, without a care.
A chill in the night, where shadows embrace,
Soft whispers of winter, a timeless space.

Silent reflections on crystalline ponds,
Drifting through twilight, where magic responds.
Every glimmering star, a hope in the dark,
Lighting the path for the dreams that embark.

Frosted horizons where visions take flight,
Carving new stories in the heart of the night.
Each moment a treasure, as time slips away,
In the cold of December, our spirits will play.

In blankets of frost, we find our retreat,
Wrapped in warm wishes, with love ever sweet.
Frigid dreams linger as the dawn drifts near,
In the hush of the night, let go of all fear.

The Glistening Dawn

When the first light breaks, the world starts to glow,
Golden hues fill the fields, soft winds gently blow.
A new day awakens, from slumber it's drawn,
Painting the heavens with the glistening dawn.

Whispers of morning, in silence they sing,
Birds join the chorus, as sunlight takes wing.
Each ray a promise, each beam a embrace,
Warming the heart in this magical space.

Dew-kissed the petals, the earth shimmering bright,
Nature's own canvas, a beautiful sight.
As shadows retreat, and the dreams take their flight,
Hope dances forward, embracing the light.

The glistening dawn, a new chapter unfolds,
With stories yet written, in sunlight embossed.
Together we rise, our hearts beating strong,
In the glow of tomorrow, where we all belong.

Glistening Traces

Beneath the moonlit sky so bright,
Softly shimmer dreams take flight.
Each moment like a fleeting star,
Guiding us, no matter how far.

Whispers linger in the air,
Tracing paths, both light and rare.
In shadows cast by silvery beams,
We chase the echoes of our dreams.

With every step on silvered ground,
Secrets of the night abound.
The world decorated with grace,
Leaves behind glistening traces.

Time weaves stories in the dark,
In the quiet, there's a spark.
A reminder in the night's embrace,
That life can be a wondrous chase.

So step lightly, feel the glow,
Of glistening traces left below.
In every heart, a whisper waits,
To guide us through these living fates.

The Cozy Hearth

In winter’s chill, a fire glows,
Where warmth and love forever flows.
The crackling wood, a gentle sound,
In this haven, peace is found.

A blanket wrapped, a cup in hand,
Bound by comfort, the heart will stand.
Stories shared as embers dance,
Moments linger in a warm romance.

Outside, the wind begins to howl,
Inside, we share a knowing scowl.
But here, beneath the flickering light,
We find our solace through the night.

The hearth, a symbol of our cheer,
Where laughter echoes, drawing near.
A sacred space to feel alive,
Where memories grow and dreams survive.

So gather close, let worries cease,
In the cozy warmth, we find our peace.
With every spark and glowing flame,
The heart ignites, never the same.

The Art of Stillness

In quiet moments, thoughts unwind,
A gentle pause, a chance to find.
The world mutes its hurried pace,
In stillness, we discover grace.

Breathe deeply in the morning light,
Embrace the calm, forget the fight.
Each heartbeat whispers tales untold,
The art of stillness, pure and bold.

Nature hums a soothing tune,
Underneath a watchful moon.
With every sigh, the mind takes flight,
In tranquil spaces, we ignite.

Feel the earth beneath your feet,
In silence, life becomes complete.
Moments stretch, like shadows cast,
In stillness, we embrace the past.

So seek the quiet, let it flow,
In stillness, wisdom starts to grow.
A canvas blank, awaiting brush,
The art of stillness, a gentle hush.

Frosty Footprints

In morning light, a world anew,
Blankets white, the sky so blue.
Frosty footprints mark the land,
Stories told with every strand.

Each step crunches in the cold,
Memories cherished, tales retold.
Beneath our feet, a whisper sings,
Of winter joys and all it brings.

Children laugh, their spirits bright,
Chasing dreams in shimmering light.
Hot cocoa waits by warming fire,
Frosty footprints never tire.

Nature sparkles, fresh and clean,
Painting scenes that feel like dreams.
Every path a journey starts,
With frosty footprints in our hearts.

So wander wide through winter's grace,
In every trace, a smile's embrace.
Let frosty footprints lead the way,
To warmth and joy in each new day.

Shiver of Dusk

The sun dips low in the sky,
Casting long shadows that sigh.
Whispers of night start to creep,
As the world drifts off to sleep.

Cool winds carry secrets untold,
As the warmth of day turns cold.
Stars flicker into the vast night,
Guiding lost souls with their light.

Colors blend in a dusky haze,
Painting the sky in twilight's glaze.
Nature breathes its evening tune,
Bathed beneath a rising moon.

Branches sway with the gentle breeze,
Rustling leaves whispering ease.
The glow of dusk wraps all around,
As peace settles without a sound.

In the stillness, time stands still,
Catching hearts with a soft thrill.
The shiver of dusk, pure and bright,
Calls us home into the night.

The Hush of Falling Snow

Silent blankets cover the ground,
Crystals fall without a sound.
Each flake tells a story to share,
In the chilly, frosty air.

Trees wear coats of shimmering white,
Embracing the calmness of night.
Footsteps crunch on the frozen earth,
Echoing laughter, joy, and mirth.

Children’s faces glow with glee,
As they shape the snow into a spree.
Snowflakes dance in the lantern's light,
Creating magic in the night.

The world pauses in tranquil grace,
In the hush, we find our place.
Every moment feels so serene,
In winter's embrace, pure and clean.

As whispers of snowflakes fall,
Nature answers the silent call.
Wrapped in wonder, hearts aglow,
We breathe in the hush of falling snow.

Crystal Veins of Time

In the quiet of a timeless void,
Lies a path often avoided.
Whispers flow like crystal streams,
Echoes of long-forgotten dreams.

Moments fracture in the light,
Reflecting shadows of the night.
Each heartbeat tells a tale profound,
In the silence, life is found.

History woven in whispering threads,
Mapping journeys where time treads.
Glimmers dance on the edge of fate,
Revealing mysteries that await.

Chronicles captured in glassy forms,
Carried by winds, through winter storms.
The pulse of ages hums a song,
Reminding us where we belong.

In the stillness, time unfolds,
Unlocking secrets that it holds.
With every tick, new hopes align,
In the crystal veins of time.

Silent Frostbite

Nights grow silent, shadows creep,
As frost begins its gentle sweep.
Biting cold that chills the bone,
In the stillness, we're alone.

Stars hang low, a chilling glow,
Whispers of winter start to flow.
Each breath comes out in a misty plume,
As silence blankets all the gloom.

Branches crack under icy weight,
Nature holds its breath, awaits.
The world seems wrapped in a tight embrace,
In this frozen, timeless space.

Softly now, the frost takes hold,
Turning warmth into stories told.
Silent frostbite, a lover's touch,
In the cold, we long for much.

As dawn breaks through the frigid night,
Morning warms the silver light.
Though frost may sting and feel unkind,
Its beauty leaves our hearts entwined.

Shadows Beneath the Boughs

Underneath the ancient trees,
Shadows dance with gentle ease.
Whispers of the evening breeze,
Secrets held in nature's keys.

Dappled light and fading sighs,
Where the stillness softly lies.
Hidden wonders, open eyes,
Magic wraps the earth in ties.

Footsteps quiet on the ground,
In this tranquil place, I'm found.
Nature’s beauty all around,
Heart and spirit, joys unbound.

Branches sway, a cradle's sway,
Time stands still, it seems to play.
In this twilight's soft decay,
Life's true essence here to stay.

Moments cherished, slow and sweet,
Here, in shadows, hearts can meet.
With each rustle, nature's beat,
In this solace, time’s retreat.

Twinkling Crystals

Stars above in velvet skies,
Twinkling bright like hopeful eyes.
Dreams that shimmer, softly rise,
In the night, the magic flies.

Moonlight bathes the world in glow,
Casting shadows, soft and slow.
Whispers of the night will flow,
Echoing where dreams will go.

Crystals glisten on the ground,
Nature’s jewels, pure and round.
In the stillness, peace is found,
With each heartbeat, joy unbound.

Raindrops catch the light's embrace,
Dancing droplets, fleeting grace.
In their flight, a freeborn trace,
Sparkling life, a warm embrace.

In the dark, the heart can soar,
Navigating through the encore.
Twinkling crystals evermore,
In the night, I seek and explore.

A Winter Reverie

Snowflakes drifting, soft and light,
Whispers of the winter night.
Blankets white, the earth in flight,
A dream wrapped in purest white.

Frosty panes, a crystal art,
Breath of winter, chilling heart.
Every moment set apart,
In this stillness, love's sweet start.

Crisp the air, a gentle bite,
Stars above, a twinkling site.
In the moon's soft, silver light,
Magic weaves through day and night.

Footprints lead through glistening snow,
Memories linger, soft and slow.
In this wonder, feelings grow,
Winter's kiss, a warm glow.

As the world in slumber lies,
Dreams emerge with winter's ties.
In the hush, a sweet surprise,
Winter’s song, a soft reprise.

Frozen Whimsy

Icicles hang from rooftops high,
Nature’s art against the sky.
Winter's breath, a gentle sigh,
Every moment, time will fly.

Children laugh in snow-clad play,
Building dreams in white array.
Sleds descend and joy holds sway,
Faces brightened, hearts in fray.

Snowmen stand with carrot nose,
Bringing smiles wherever goes.
In the chill, a warmth bestows,
Fleeting moments, time bestows.

Caught in twirls of swirling flakes,
Every breath, the stillness wakes.
Frozen wonder, joy thus takes,
In this bliss, my heart awakes.

When the sun begins to rise,
Glittering jewels mesmerize.
Nature's spell, a sweet surprise,
Frozen whimsy, life’s reprise.

Twinkling Snowfall

The snowflakes dance in light,
A shimmer of pure delight.
Gentle whispers fill the air,
Nature's art beyond compare.

Each flake tells a tale so bright,
Underneath the pale moonlight.
Softly drifting, taking flight,
A fleeting dream, a snowy sight.

They blanket earth in quiet peace,
In their charm, all troubles cease.
Every sparkle, earth adorned,
In their magic, hearts reborn.

As dawn breaks with soft gold hue,
The world awakens, fresh and new.
In the stillness, magic glows,
A wonderland where beauty flows.

Twinkling snow, pure as can be,
Holds the secrets of the sea.
In its grace, our spirits soar,
Through the winter, forevermore.

Secrets in the Snow

Beneath the blanket, whispers lie,
Secrets held where shadows sigh.
Each footprint tells of tales untold,
In winter’s grip, the world feels bold.

Golden dreams in silver frost,
Memories linger, never lost.
In every drift, a story sleeps,
In every silence, mystery creeps.

As snowflakes fall, they softly weave,
Fragile hopes that we believe.
In solitude, we find our way,
Through the cold light of winter's day.

With every storm, a truth unfolds,
In chilling winds, the heart holds.
The quiet snow that drapes the ground,
Hides the wonders yet unbound.

Secrets rest in layers deep,
In the hushed white, promise keeps.
Listen closely, hear the song,
In the snow, we all belong.

Songs of the Frozen

In the silence, songs arise,
Melodies beneath gray skies.
Winter whispers with each breath,
A hymn of life beyond the death.

Icicles glisten, shining bright,
Singing softly in the night.
Every flake a note to play,
A frozen symphony at bay.

Echoes of the past return,
In the hearth, the embers burn.
With each chill, the spirits soar,
In the frost, we crave much more.

Melancholy, yet so sweet,
In winter's grasp, our hearts repeat.
The beauty of the frozen lands,
In harmony, the world expands.

Songs of warmth in bitter cold,
Stories of the brave and bold.
In the frost's embrace we find,
The music that connects mankind.

Sighs of the Frost

The trees lined up in still repose,
With coats of white, like winter’s prose.
Every breath a frosty sigh,
As chilly winds begin to fly.

The earth beneath, so crisp and bare,
In frozen thoughts, we linger there.
Each gust carries a secret tale,
Tales of love that will prevail.

With every chill, a heartbeat missed,
In the hour where dreams persist.
The softest touch of winter’s grace,
Leaves traces on this quiet space.

As shadows stretch and daylight wanes,
The night reveals the frost's remains.
In moonlight's glow, we find our peace,
In silence deep, our doubts release.

Sighs of the frost, whispering low,
Reminding us of the world’s slow flow.
In winter's grasp, we find our way,
In each sigh, a prayer, we say.

When Silence Sleeps

When silence sleeps, the world takes pause,
Thoughts drift slowly without a cause.
In the quiet, dreams softly sing,
Whispers of peace that the night will bring.

Stars blanket the sky in their soft embrace,
Time holds its breath in this sacred space.
Echoes of laughter linger like mist,
In the heart of stillness, moments persist.

Each shadow dances, a fleeting glow,
While the moonlight bathes all below.
Hearts wrapped in calm, the night unfolds,
Secrets of twilight in stories untold.

Forgotten worries fade with the light,
In the cocoon of dark, everything feels right.
As dawn approaches, dreams take flight,
But in this stillness, the soul ignites.

When silence sleeps, the world renews,
In every breath, a hidden muse.
Let tranquility fill the air, so deep,
For in the silence, our hearts will keep.

Veils of Ice and Snow

Veils of ice and snow drift down,
Softly cloaking the sleeping town.
Winter whispers in the gentle breeze,
Nature's magic wrapped in freeze.

Each flake a star from the frigid sky,
Landing lightly, where dreams lie.
Cold breath dances on frozen streams,
Creating wonders like porcelain dreams.

Trees wear coats of shimmering white,
A landscape transformed, pure and bright.
Footprints linger on the icy ground,
In a world where silence is profound.

The night falls softly, a velvet shroud,
Beneath a quilt, the earth is proud.
In this realm where time stands still,
We find solace; the heart’s sweet thrill.

Veils of ice and snow embrace,
Wrapping the world in a tender grace.
In winter's hold, we find a way,
To cherish the warmth of every day.

A Chill in the Air

A chill in the air, whispers of frost,
Nature exhales, the warmth is lost.
Leaves tremble gently, bids farewell,
As shadows of winter begin to swell.

Golden sunsets fade into gray,
Fleeting moments of bright decay.
The sky dons a cloak of twilight blue,
While the moon peeks out, shy and new.

In every breath, a puff of smoke,
Unraveling secrets that winter spoke.
With every step, crunches beneath,
Tell stories of life in the cold beneath.

Fires burn brightly, warmth we seek,
Comfort in company, hearts to speak.
As stars twinkle in the frozen gloom,
In warmth of kinship, our spirits bloom.

A chill in the air, but hearts are bold,
In winter's embrace, our stories unfold.
With every sunset, the promise remains,
That spring will return to break these chains.

Solstice Soliloquy

In the depths of night, the solstice calls,
A moment where time in silence falls.
Stars gather close, their secrets to share,
As we ponder the dreams that linger in air.

The longest night wraps us in dreams,
While shadows flicker by candle beams.
Whispers of winter in a soft refrain,
Breath held close to escape the pain.

Gathered around the blazing fire,
Hearts intertwine, rising higher.
Stories shared of the year gone by,
In the glow of embers, laughter will fly.

The world pauses, in reverie deep,
While the earth begins to gently weep.
For in the darkness, we find a spark,
A promise of light to banish the dark.

Solstice soliloquy, a timeless tale,
In the embrace of night, we shall not fail.
For with every end, a beginning anew,
In the balance of night, we start to break through.

Silent Landscapes

In the hush of dawn, shadows lay,
Whispers of dreams in the soft gray.
Mountains stand tall, cloaked in white,
Nature holds breath, a tranquil sight.

Crystal streams weave through the pines,
Glistening jewels, nature’s designs.
Birds take flight, their songs arise,
Echoes of peace beneath vast skies.

Morning light scatters through trees,
Dancing with leaves in the gentle breeze.
Every path, a story untold,
Silent landscapes in beauty unfold.

The world awakes, colors ignite,
A canvas painted in soft daylight.
Footsteps wander on trails so wide,
In silent landscapes, we confide.

Time drifts softly, moments freeze,
Fragile and precious as autumn leaves.
In this stillness, hearts find their beat,
In silent landscapes, life feels complete.

A Flurry of Thoughts

Whirlwinds dance through my busy mind,
Fragmented pieces, unconfined.
Like paper scattered, tossed by wind,
A flurry of thoughts that never rescind.

Questions linger, answers evade,
Waves of doubt, a mental cascade.
Each fleeting moment, a butterfly's flight,
A flurry of thoughts in chaotic sight.

Ideas collide like stars in space,
Flickering visions that leave their trace.
In the silence, inspiration breeds,
A flurry of thoughts turns into deeds.

Night descends, quiet embraces,
Calm descends as the day erases.
In the stillness, clarity shines,
A flurry of thoughts, now defined lines.

Once tangled webs are gently spun,
From chaos, calm is finally won.
With each heartbeat, the chatter slows,
A flurry of thoughts softly goes.

Threads of Ice

Delicate patterns weave through the night,
Frosted whispers, a spectacular sight.
Nature's fingers stretch wide and pure,
Threads of ice that softly allure.

Under the moon, the world seems still,
Each glittering edge, a graceful thrill.
Crystalline shores where silence reigns,
Threads of ice, like delicate chains.

Amid the chill, warmth is found,
The heart beats softly, a gentle sound.
In tranquil moments, the spirit flows,
Threads of ice, where harmony grows.

Season's embrace, a frosty kiss,
Wrapped in magic, we find our bliss.
With every dawn, a new surprise,
Threads of ice under warming skies.

Transience weaves through the winter air,
Moments held close, a whispered prayer.
In fragile beauty, life intertwines,
Threads of ice as the sunlight shines.

Hidden Beneath the Snow

Beneath the surface, secrets sleep,
Wonders of nature, buried deep.
In the cloak of winter, stillness flows,
Whispers of life, hidden beneath the snow.

Silent slumbers in cold embrace,
Roots entwined in their frozen place.
Patterns of life, waiting to show,
Mysteries hidden beneath the snow.

The world slows down, a gentle pause,
Winter's power, nature’s cause.
Each flake a promise, a gift in tow,
Stories await, hidden beneath the snow.

Silent growth through the chilling night,
Hope lies dormant, longing for light.
With each thaw, a new tale will grow,
Revealing treasures hidden below.

As spring approaches, life stirs anew,
Painting the earth in vibrant hue.
From slumber's grip, life starts to flow,
Unveiling wonders hidden beneath the snow.

The Language of Ice

Whispers of silence fill the air,
Glaciers gleam with an ancient glare.
Frozen tales etched in cold,
Nature's secrets slowly unfold.

Crystalline patterns drift and glide,
Cascading down where shadows hide.
Each shard a story, sharp yet bright,
A language written in the night.

Beneath the weight of frosty dreams,
Echoes of life in icy beams.
The world transforms, a pale embrace,
In every crevice, beauty's grace.

Snowflakes dance like whispers fair,
Each one unique, spun with care.
Together they weave a winter's tale,
A soft enchantment, a tranquil veil.

As twilight gathers, shadows grow,
The language of ice begins to glow.
With every flake that falls in pure,
A promise of magic, cold and sure.

Twilight in the Snow

The dusk descends on fields of white,
A canvas brushed with fading light.
Silhouettes dance, shadows stretch wide,
In twilight's glow, the world confides.

Stars awaken, softly they gleam,
Nestled 'neath the frosty seam.
Each flake glistens, a diamond's kiss,
In winter's arms, there's tranquil bliss.

Footprints whisper, tales left behind,
A journey shared with heart and mind.
Through frozen woods, the paths entwine,
As whispers call from pine to pine.

Crimson hues in the sky's embrace,
Mark the end of day with grace.
As snowflakes swirl in a gentle waltz,
Time slows down, our worries halt.

With evening’s charm, the chill grows deep,
Wrapped in cozy dreams we keep.
Beneath the moon's soft, silver glow,
We find our peace in twilight's snow.

Soft Crystals

Delicate forms in the winter’s air,
Soft crystals shimmer, light as prayer.
Each one unique, a fragile bloom,
Transforming silence into zoom.

They flutter down from clouds above,
A gentle kiss from sky to dove.
Nature’s artwork, a fleeting glance,
A moment’s magic, a winter's dance.

Lining the branches, wrapping the ground,
In quiet corners, beauty is found.
Whispers of winter, soft and sweet,
Their charm enchants with each heartbeat.

In sparkling blankets, dreams unfurl,
A frosty canvas, a shimmering world.
Glimmers of sunlight, each facet bright,
Soft crystals twinkle with pure delight.

As day breaks forth, they softly fade,
Yet memories linger, never abate.
In the heart of winter, still they remain,
A testament to magic, sweet refrain.

Enchanted Frost

A carpet woven with glistening lace,
Enchanted frost, a timeless grace.
Each blade of grass, a jeweled star,
Whispers of winter from near and far.

Underneath the moon's soft sigh,
The world transforms as night drifts by.
Each breath of wind, a ghostly tune,
In the embrace of a silvered moon.

Icicles hang like chandeliers bright,
Glittering softly in the night.
Nature's jewels, in pristine cheer,
A frosty kingdom that draws us near.

In the stillness, magic reigns,
A tranquil peace that solitude gains.
With every touch, the cold ignites,
Enchanted frost in starry nights.

As dawn approaches, colors blend,
Yet in our hearts, the frost won't end.
For every flake, a story spun,
In frosty wonder, we are all one.

Shivers in Stillness

In the quiet, shadows crawl,
Breath of winter, a distant call.
Frosty whispers weave through the night,
Where dreams dance in pale moonlight.

Each heartbeat echoes in the cold,
Tales of warmth in silence told.
Branches creak, a lullaby,
As stars flicker, a distant sigh.

The air hangs thick, a gentle pause,
Nature's grip, with no applause.
Stillness settles like soft snow,
In the hush, secrets flow.

Footsteps falter on the ground,
Lost in peace, without a sound.
Veils of twilight softly blend,
In the stillness, find my friend.

Time unravels, slow and deep,
In shadows where the memories keep.
A moment caught, forever still,
In shivers, find a quiet thrill.

Ethereal Hush

Whispers linger in the air,
A soft embrace, a gentle care.
Through the stillness, echoes glide,
In the silence, dreams reside.

Moonlit paths on velvet ground,
Lost in beauty, peace profound.
Stars awaken, twinkle bright,
In the depths of velvet night.

Laughter dances on the breeze,
Carried softly through the trees.
Time dissolves, leaving no trace,
In the hush, we find our place.

Shadows merge, a fleeting blend,
Every corner hides a friend.
Tender moments, softly spun,
In ethereal silence, we are one.

A gentle sigh, the world takes pause,
In this hush, we find our cause.
Chasing dreams on starlit streams,
In the stillness, wake our dreams.

Crystal Silence

In the dawn's first gentle light,
Glittering frost, a wondrous sight.
Branches hold their crystal tears,
Silent stories of all our years.

Each breath we take, a fleeting sound,
Whispers glisten all around.
Time stands still, the world changed hue,
In this crystal silence, only you.

Footsteps soft on snowy ground,
Magic lingers all around.
Every heartbeat feels alive,
In this quiet, we thrive.

Cobwebs shine in morning's glow,
Nature's art in winter's flow.
A moment caught, a timeless dance,
In silence, our hearts enhance.

With every glance, we hold the day,
In crystal beauty, hearts will sway.
Eternity rests in the calm,
In this stillness, find the balm.

Subtle Chill

A breath of cool whispers near,
Soft and gentle, drawing near.
In the twilight, shadows spread,
Subtle chills, where dreams are fed.

Clouds gather like thoughts in flight,
Painting the canvas of night.
With every gust, we feel alive,
In the chill, our spirits thrive.

The world transforms under the stars,
Fading echoes of distant cars.
Wrapped in warmth, yet feeling free,
In subtle chill, just you and me.

Frosty air brings clarity,
Moments float in simplicity.
Here we pause, let worries cease,
In this chill, we find our peace.

With laughter mingling in the night,
Subtle, soft, the world feels right.
Embraced by cool, we seek and find,
In the stillness, hearts aligned.

Frosty Mornings

The dawn breaks clear and bright,
With frost upon the ground.
Trees glisten in the light,
A silent, chilly sound.

Breath clouds in the crisp air,
Each step a gentle crunch.
The world seems draped in care,
As nature takes her lunch.

Birds whisper soft and low,
Their wings brushing the freeze.
Winter's gentle show,
Brings hearts a sweet unease.

Sunrise dances on the ice,
Casting jewels everywhere.
Time drifts, a gentle slice,
Of beauty beyond compare.

These frosty mornings hum,
With secrets left untold.
In nature's frozen drum,
Life's wonders unfold.

Dreaming in Ice

In dreams where shadows play,
The whispers swirl like snow.
Each thought drifts far away,
In winter's frosty glow.

Crystals form and take shape,
A world of pure delight.
Within this icy drape,
Hope dances in the night.

Winds weave through the trees,
A lullaby so sweet.
As dreams ride on the breeze,
Each moment feels complete.

Frozen rivers gleam bright,
Reflecting silver stars.
In the heart of the night,
We scribble our memoirs.

Awake within this dream,
Where ice and heart collide.
In this ethereal theme,
Our spirits freely glide.

The Calm Before Spring

The earth holds its breath tight,
In stillness, shadows lay.
Frost blankets the night,
Before bright blooms hold sway.

A hush drapes all around,
As life begins to stir.
Winter's soft, silent sound,
Leaves whispers, faint and pure.

The sky blushes with hope,
In tints of pastel hue.
Nature learns to elope,
From the cold, bleak adieu.

Buds peek from their retreat,
Defying icy chains.
Awakening so sweet,
Where warmth replaces pains.

This calm before the change,
A promise held so near.
Each moment feels so strange,
Yet bright with love and cheer.

Echoes of the Frigid Night

Beneath a starry shroud,
The night echoes so clear.
Whispers drift like a cloud,
A melody to hear.

Chill air wraps around me,
As shadows dance and sway.
The moon, a watchful key,
Unlocks the night's bouquet.

Footsteps crunch on the frost,
Each sound a winding tale.
In silence, we are lost,
Where dreams and hopes prevail.

The world seems far away,
Yet close within our hearts.
In echoes, we will stay,
As night and day departs.

A symphony of cold,
In each twinkling glance given.
In stillness, we behold,
The path that we have risen.

Beneath the Ice

Underneath the frozen lake,
Secrets whisper, still and deep.
Silent dreams that softly wake,
In the night, where shadows creep.

Icicles like crystal spears,
Guard the tales of ages past.
Time stands still through winter's years,
In the silence, thoughts are cast.

Cold winds sing a haunting song,
Echoes dance across the white.
Beneath the surface, life is strong,
Hidden gems in dark's delight.

Frozen world, a mystic maze,
Nature paints with silver brush.
In the twilight's quiet haze,
Feel the heartbeat, feel the hush.

Beneath the ice, a breathless sigh,
Moments sealed in winter's clasp.
Where the echoes softly die,
In the stillness, dreams we grasp.

Symphonies of Solitude

In the stillness, silence reigns,
Whispers linger in the air.
Notes of longing, soft refrains,
Floating lightly, unaware.

Alone beneath the starry veil,
Heartbeats blend with nature's hum.
In this peace, no fears prevail,
Melodies, elusive, come.

Moonlit shadows stretch and sway,
Dancing softly on the ground.
In the night, they drift away,
Lost in echoes, profound sound.

Every breath a tender chord,
Played by winds that gently sigh.
Symphonies in solitude,
As the world goes drifting by.

In this moment, I am free,
Wrapped in warmth of quiet grace.
Here, the heart finds harmony,
In loneliness, a sacred space.

The Heart of Cold

In the frost where stillness dwells,
Beat of winter, slow and true.
Nature weaves her wintry spells,
In the white, a world anew.

Breath of ice upon the land,
Frigid whispers, soft and pure.
Touched by snow, the earth does stand,
Silent beauty, calm and sure.

Underneath the crystal sky,
Life's resilience echoes strong.
Where the frozen rivers lie,
In the heart, it beats along.

Every flake a tale retold,
Of the seasons' endless dance.
In the chill, we find the bold,
Seeking warmth in nature's glance.

In the depths where cold resides,
A light flickers, warm and bright.
The heart of cold, where love abides,
In the shadows, there is light.

Glimmers of Frost

Morning breaks with crystal rays,
Glimmers sparkling, pure and bright.
On the grass, like diamonds' praise,
In the dawn's early light.

Nature shimmers, worlds awake,
Every breath a frosty dance.
On the lake, reflections break,
In the beauty, lost in trance.

Touch of winter's gentle breath,
Painting pictures, soft and grand.
In the silence, hints of death,
Yet renewal stirs, so planned.

Time flows on, yet still we pause,
To embrace these fleeting sights.
In the frost, a moment's cause,
Caught in nature's soft delights.

Glimmers fade as day takes chase,
Yet they linger in the mind.
Echoes of a frozen grace,
In the heart, their warmth we find.

Icy Murmurs

The winter winds softly sigh,
In the silence, echoes lie.
Snowflakes dance under the moon,
A chilling, gentle tune.

Branches bend under weight's care,
Crystals glint, beyond compare.
Each breath a ghost in the air,
Nature's heart, raw and bare.

Along the stream, ice does cling,
Whispers of frost, the cold brings.
Time seems to pause, it stands still,
A quietness that can thrill.

Footsteps crunch on frozen ground,
Echoes of stillness abound.
In this realm, peace intertwines,
With the cold, a warmth aligns.

Icy murmurs call the night,
Guiding souls to soft twilight.
Nature's secrets softly bloom,
In shadows, a silver gloom.

A Season for Stillness

The world slows down in the frost,
In this stillness, time is lost.
Blankets of snow hush the sound,
In quiet, beauty is found.

Each breath hangs like a soft sigh,
Under the pale, slate-gray sky.
Trees wear crowns of shimmering white,
Holding secrets of the night.

Stars peek out with a gentle glow,
Guiding hearts through the snow.
Each flake a tale, unique and rare,
A season to pause, to care.

Moments stretch in cool embrace,
Nature's peace, a sacred space.
In each whisper, stories told,
A season for stillness, pure gold.

As dawn breaks, hues softly blend,
In silence, the echoes mend.
A canvas painted with grace,
The world finds its proper place.

Frost-kissed Whispers

Morning light on crystal clear,
Frost-kissed whispers, draw near.
Nature’s breath, pure and bright,
Songs of winter take flight.

Each branch adorned with icy lace,
Holds the chill of nature's grace.
Whispers float on gentle air,
A hint of magic everywhere.

Beneath the trees, shadows play,
Caught in the light of day.
The world a glimmering sight,
Wrapped in the warmth of light.

In the stillness, hearts convene,
Finding peace in the serene.
With every step, a soft kiss,
Frosted tales of winter bliss.

As sunlight fades, the colors glow,
Frost-kissed whispers continue to flow.
In the twilight, calm descends,
Nature's songs never end.

Whispering Pines

Tall and proud, the pines stand still,
Whispering secrets, strong and shrill.
In the breezes, tales take flight,
Nature's heart is pure delight.

Their needles dance in twilight's glow,
Guardians of dreams, they know.
Each rustle tells of ages past,
A symphony, both vast and fast.

Under their boughs, shadows play,
Softened light at the end of day.
A sanctuary where souls get lost,
In each moment, count the cost.

Whispering winds through branches weave,
In their embrace, one can believe.
Hope's gentle touch, a tender sign,
Life's a journey, the stars align.

As starlight spills on the earth's face,
The pines continue their quiet grace.
In their whispers, a world reborn,
Awakens with each new dawn.

Shadows of Snow

Soft whispers coat the ground,
A blanket of white all around.
Footsteps crunch with muted sound,
In winter's grip, peace is found.

Trees stand tall with arms of frost,
They guard the warmth that seems all lost.
The world, in silence, bears its cost,
Yet in this chill, no love's a gloss.

Moonlight dances on the drifts,
A silver shimmer that gently shifts.
Each shadow sings, its spirit lifts,
In freezing air, the stillness gifts.

Nature wrapped in calm embrace,
Each flake a story, soft in grace.
The night is long, yet we find space,
To dream beneath the snow's own lace.

Through every flurry, laughter flows,
In joy, the heart forever glows.
In shadows deep, our love still grows,
Bound by the world that winter shows.

Hushed Nature

Amidst the calm, the silence reigns,
Nature whispers softly, free from chains.
In gentle hues, the world remains,
A cradle rocked where peace sustains.

Leaves flutter down like thoughts anew,
Each breath a gift, each moment true.
The sun peeks softly, bright, and blue,
In hush of dawn, all life imbues.

Mountains echo the quiet light,
A canvas painted, pure delight.
In hidden glades, the day turns bright,
As shadows blend with morning’s flight.

Crickets hum in twilight’s song,
In every note, we all belong.
The night unfolds, mysterious, strong,
In every hush, our dreams prolong.

Awake the stars, they fill the sky,
A silent crowd that never lies.
In nature's heart, we find the why,
Where every breath is a soft sigh.

Crystal Tranquility

A crystal stream flows soft and clear,
Reflecting light that draws us near.
The tranquil sound, a song we hear,
In gentle waves, we shed our fear.

Pebbles lie like jewels bestowed,
Each turn revealing nature's code.
In depths of blue, our worries erode,
In calm embrace, we share the road.

Willows weep in graceful poise,
Their leaves a whisper, nature's voice.
In softest breaths, the world rejoices,
A haven found where heart choices.

Beneath the canopy of green,
The air is filled with sights unseen.
In every rustle, life's routine,
A tranquil moment, sweet and clean.

Night descends with stars in tow,
Crystal dreams begin to flow.
In quietude, we come to know,
The beauty found in every glow.

Beneath the White Veil

Beneath the veil of purest white,
A world transformed in soft twilight.
The frozen earth, a wondrous sight,
In winter's cloak, the heart takes flight.

Each branch adorned with crystal lace,
A fleeting moment, time and space.
Where whispers linger, warmth's embrace,
In hush of snow, we find our place.

Frost-kissed paths hide secrets deep,
Where echoes play, and shadows creep.
In every silence, memories seep,
A dreamlike state, inviting sleep.

Horizon glows with blush of dawn,
A promise born as night is gone.
In softest hues, the day moves on,
Beneath the veil, life’s magic drawn.

So let us wander, hand in hand,
Through winter's realm, this snowy land.
In every flake, a story planned,
Beneath the white veil, we will stand.

Frost-kissed Serenade

In the hush of early dawn,
Whispers of frost on the lawn.
Nature's blanket, soft and white,
Holds the world in pure delight.

Each breath a cloud, chilled and slow,
As winter's magic starts to glow.
Trees wear coats of sparkling sheen,
Silent beauty, calm and clean.

Footsteps crunch on frozen ground,
Echoes dance, a joyous sound.
Children laugh, their spirits high,
Beneath the vast and azure sky.

As daylight fades, stars emerge,
In the night, soft shadows surge.
Moonlight glimmers on the snow,
Painting dreams in silver glow.

Embrace the night, the chill, the peace,
In this moment, worries cease.
Frost-kissed serenade of bliss,
Winter's heart, a tranquil kiss.

Chilling Breath of Silence

A quiet breath, the air so still,
Icicles hang from every hill.
Frosted whispers fill the night,
Moonlit paths glow, pure and bright.

The world wrapped in icy lace,
Nature dons a tranquil face.
Snowflakes drift with gentle grace,
In this frozen, silent space.

Stars above twinkle like gems,
While shadows loom on frozen stems.
The chilling breath, a calm embrace,
A timeless pause, a soft trace.

In the distance, a lone owl sings,
As winter's peace spreads its wings.
All is serene, all is still,
In the heart of winter's chill.

Embrace the night, savor the calm,
In the stillness, find your balm.
Chilling breath, a whispering song,
In this moment, you belong.

Snowbound Secrets

Underneath the blankets deep,
Silent stories lie in sleep.
Footprints fade in powdery white,
Disguised secrets, out of sight.

Whispers carried on the breeze,
Hidden tales of ancient trees.
Snowdrifts mask the paths we roam,
In this quiet, we find home.

Frost-kissed air, a gentle plea,
Nature's wonder, wild and free.
Beneath the surface, magic lies,
In the twilight, truth belies.

Softly falls the moonlit snow,
Layered histories start to show.
Each flake a tale waiting to bloom,
In winter’s vast, enchanted room.

Snowbound secrets, held so dear,
In the silence, they draw near.
Listen closely, hear their call,
In the stillness, find it all.

Icicle Lullabies

Icicles dangle, sharp and cold,
Winter's touch is pure, bold.
Glistening gems on rooftops cling,
Nature's melody starts to sing.

Softly falls the crystal snow,
Sways upon the wind, aglow.
Each flake a note, a gentle sigh,
In the vast, unending sky.

Winter's breath, a quiet tune,
Nights adorned with stars and moon.
Beneath the night, dreams arise,
Cradled in these lullabies.

Frosty whispers, sweet and light,
Cradle hearts in silent night.
Every twinkle, every glow,
Sings of peace in fields below.

Icicle lullabies hum low,
In the stillness, warm and slow.
Let the melody draw you near,
In winter's embrace, feel no fear.

A Tapestry of White

In silence falls the gentle snow,
A blanket soft, a quiet glow.
Each flake a tale, each drift a dream,
A world transformed, a silver seam.

Trees wear coats of sparkling frost,
The warmth within seems so embossed.
Whispers dance on chilled, crisp air,
A magic weave beyond compare.

Footprints trace where lovers tread,
Through whispered woods where dreams are fed.
Nestled paths in winter's arms,
In every curve, in every charm.

Beneath the moon, the shadows play,
A symphony of night and day.
The stars they twinkle, bright and clear,
In this tapestry, we hold dear.

So let the cold embrace the heart,
For in this white, we find our art.
In every stitch of winter's lace,
A fleeting moment we embrace.

The Serpent of Snow

Slithering softly, the serpent winds,
Through valleys deep where silence binds.
It coils around each hidden space,
A whispering ghost, a secret grace.

Glistening scales of purest white,
Reflect the day, absorb the night.
Where shadows linger, it will creep,
In frozen realms where dreams still sleep.

With every twist, a story grows,
Of ancient woods and frozen flows.
It beckons softly, draws us near,
In chilling dance, there's naught to fear.

The breath of winter fills the air,
As thoughts entwine in sacred prayer.
For in the quiet, there’s a sound,
A melody where peace is found.

Oh serpent sleek, weave us your song,
In your embrace, we all belong.
Through winter’s grasp, we find our way,
In dreams of snow, our hearts will stay.

Hidden Paths of Ice

A path obscured, the ice concealed,
With every step, a fate revealed.
Beneath the frosted, glassy sheen,
Lies hidden magic, soft and green.

Twists and turns of nature’s art,
Calling forth the wandering heart.
In crystal corridors we roam,
While shadows whisper tales of home.

Bright stars above, a twinkling guide,
Through frozen woods, we choose to stride.
Each brittle branch, a wondrous sight,
A hint of warmth in winter’s bite.

Voices echo in the night,
A symphony of pure delight.
We follow where the cold winds lead,
On hidden paths, our spirits freed.

At dawn’s first light, the frost will break,
Unraveled dreams, a path we make.
With trust in each frozen embrace,
We find our strength, we find our place.

Glacial Thoughts

In icy depths where silence rests,
Our thoughts are still, like frozen quests.
Each moment carved in crystal form,
A tranquil pulse, a calming warm.

Waves of blue, like lucid skies,
Reflecting truths, where wisdom lies.
Each glimmer holds a secret thought,
In depths of ice, our dreams are caught.

The stillness speaks, a voice so clear,
In contemplation, we draw near.
With every breath, the chill enchants,
As glacial hearts begin to dance.

Thoughts shimmer like the morning light,
In quietude, they take their flight.
Through icy realms where spirits soar,
In glacial thoughts, we search for more.

So let us wander, free and bold,
In avenues where dreams unfold.
With glacial grace, we find our way,
In realms of thought, our hearts will stay.

Frosted Echoes

In the hush of winter's breath,
Whispers dance on frozen air.
Footprints fade in icy depth,
Silent tales of warmth laid bare.

Trees wear coats of glittering white,
Nature's jewels, a wondrous sight.
The world transformed, pure delight,
As stars embrace the velvet night.

Crisp and clear, the moonlight flows,
Painting dreams on frost-kissed ground.
Echoes linger, soft and slow,
In this tranquil joy, we're found.

Winter's song, a gentle hum,
Calls the heart to pause and feel.
In the quiet, shadows come,
Frosted echoes, ever real.

As dawn creeps in, the glow awakes,
Golden warmth begins to rise.
But in the chill, the spirit shakes,
Frosted echoes, our sweet prize.

Silvery Veils

In twilight's kiss, a veil is cast,
A silvery shimmer on the land.
Each breath of chill, it whispers past,
Enfolding all with gentle hand.

Beneath the sky, so vast and deep,
The world creates a shivering art.
In every corner, secrets keep,
Silvery veils, a winter's heart.

Night's embrace, so dark, so light,
Frost on branches, delicate lace.
Stars emerge in soft, first light,
In this quiet, find your place.

Windswept echoes call us near,
To frosty paths that twist and twine.
We wander where the heart holds dear,
The silvery veils that intertwine.

A silence wrapped in crystalline,
Nature's breath on the frozen ground.
In this moment, all is fine,
Silvery veils, a love profound.

Chilling Reverie

When shadows stretch and daylight wanes,
A chilling reverie takes flight.
The breath of frost, like whispered chains,
Holds the world in gentle night.

Glimmers soft on fields of gray,
Where dreams are born from winter's hush.
In the glow of twilight's play,
A heart finds peace in nature's brush.

Winds weave tales of yesteryear,
As echoes rise from silent ground.
In the stillness, memories steer,
Chilling reverie, love profound.

The world wraps tight in blankets cold,
While stars spill secrets, crisp and bright.
Every story gently told,
As darkness dances with the light.

So let us walk through frosty dreams,
In reveries where silence reigns.
With each step, the heart redeems,
Chilling whispers, love remains.

The Quiet Cold

In the stillness of the night,
The quiet cold begins to creep.
Softly veiling all in white,
Wrapped in layers, secrets keep.

A frosty breath upon my skin,
The world outside holds its breath tight.
In the heart, a warmth within,
While winter plays in snowy flight.

Branches bow with silver grace,
Covered in a frosty crown.
Time slows down in this embrace,
The quiet cold, a tender gown.

Stars wink through the veil of night,
Their shimmer dances on the snow.
A world transformed in purest light,
The quiet cold, a gentle glow.

So let the silence wrap you close,
In the hush where dreams take hold.
Nature's peace, a calming dose,
In the depths of the quiet cold.

Echoes in the Frost

In the stillness, whispers weave,
Frozen secrets, hearts believe.
Echoes linger through the night,
Moonbeams dance in silver light.

Footprints trace the path of dreams,
Softly swaying, nature seems.
Trees adorned with icy lace,
A tranquil, cold, enchanted space.

Chill of dawn upon the ground,
Silent breaths, all around.
Nature's voice in soft refrain,
Frosty kisses, sweet as rain.

In the quiet, time stands still,
Echoes captured, winter's thrill.
Colors fade to muted gray,
Yet the heart warms in this play.

Glistening Shadows of December

Glistening shadows dance and sway,
In the dusk of winter's day.
Crystal flakes in twilight fall,
Whispers soft, a silent call.

Branches bow beneath the weight,
Nature holds her breath, sedate.
Stars emerge in velvet skies,
Telling tales with twinkling eyes.

Fires crackle with tales of old,
Hearts are warm, though nights are cold.
Memories wrapped in woolen threads,
In every heart, a story spreads.

Snowflakes twirl in moon's embrace,
Time lost in this sacred space.
Every shadow tells a tale,
Of winter's sweep, of nature's sail.

The Tundra's Caress

Under skies of deepest blue,
Tundra sleeps, a tranquil view.
Crystal fields stretch far and wide,
Nature’s breath, a gentle guide.

Whispers echo through the haze,
Crisp and clear, the heart obeys.
Solitude in frozen grace,
Time stands still in this embrace.

The horizon, a canvas bright,
Sunrise blooms, igniting light.
In the still, the soul takes flight,
Tundra’s warmth a pure delight.

Every breath a frosty cheer,
Moments linger, crystal clear.
Nature sings, a soft caress,
In the tundra’s vast wilderness.

Cold Whispers in the Moonlight

Cold whispers call from shadows deep,
Through the night, the secrets creep.
Silver beams on tranquil snow,
Gentle sighs in breezes blow.

Stars like diamonds, bright and clear,
Dancing softly, drawing near.
Moonlit paths lead hearts astray,
In the silence, dreams hold sway.

Frosted air, a tender kiss,
In this night, we find our bliss.
Nature's lullaby in flight,
Softly sung in whispered light.

Every shadow tells of peace,
In the calm, our hopes increase.
Cold whispers warm the winter night,
Guided by the moon's soft light.

Milton Keynes UK
Ingram Content Group UK Ltd.
UKHW021402081224
452111UK00007B/120

9 789916 797860